YES, PLEASE!

NO, THANK YOU!

VALERIE WHEELER

ILLUSTRATED BY **GLIN DIBLEY**

STERLING PUBLISHING CO., INC.
NEW YORK

To Ryan and Quinn, with love.
—V.W.

This for my dear friends Kim,
Dave and Drew Silva.
—G.D.

Library of Congress Cataloging-in-Publication Data Available

2   4   6   8   10   9   7   5   3

Published by Sterling Publishing Co., Inc.

387 Park Avenue South, New York, NY 10016

Text copyright © 2005 by Valerie Wheeler

Illustrations copyright © 2005 by Glin Dibley

Distributed in Canada by Sterling Publishing

c/o Canadian Manda Group, 165 Dufferin Street

Toronto, Ontario, Canada M6K 3H6

Distributed in Great Britain and Europe by Chris Lloyd at Orca Book

Services, Stanley House, Fleets Lane, Poole BH15 3AJ, England

Distributed in Australia by Capricorn Link (Australia) Pty. Ltd.

P.O. Box 704, Windsor, NSW 2756, Australia

Printed in China

Sterling ISBN 1-4027-1746-6

For information about custom editions, special sales, premium and

corporate purchases, please contact Sterling Special Sales

Department at 800-805-5489 or specialsales@sterlingpub.com.

I have a game for you to play
about how you can spend your day.
I'll ask you what you'd like to do.
You'll say "Yes, please!" or "No, thank you!"

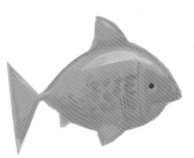

Would you like to swim in the ocean
on the back of a dolphin?

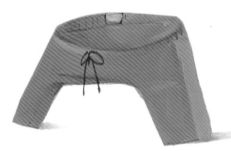

Would you like that dolphin to steal
your bathing suit?

Would you like to get everything you
want at the toy store?

Would you like to carry all your toys
home by yourself?

Would you like to go galloping on
a pony?

Would you like to spend the rest of
the day cleaning out the pony stalls?

Would you like to take a trip to the
North Pole?

Would you like to forget your coat
and mittens?

Would you like to visit the fair and
go on rides?

Would you like to throw up on the
lady beside you?

Would you like to go to the fire station and play on the trucks?

Would you like to get soaked by the
fire hose?

Would you like to have a big party
with all of your friends?

Would you like to clean up after the party all by yourself?

Would you like to play "Yes, please! No, thank you!" some more?